THE ETCHINGS OF CANALETTO

by Jacob Kainen   *The Smithsonian Press · Washington, D.C. 1967*

SMITHSONIAN PUBLICATION 4676. DESIGNED BY CRIMILDA PONTES

LIBRARY OF CONGRESS CATALOG CARD NUMBER: 67-19731

PRODUCED BY THE MERIDEN GRAVURE COMPANY

AND THE STINEHOUR PRESS.

The following essay was originally intended for a catalog to accompany an exhibition at the **_Foreword_**
Division of Graphic Arts of the United States National Museum. Held in the autumn of
1965, the exhibition included all thirty-one of Canaletto's published etchings, which were
acquired through the generosity of Mrs. Frances P. Garvan of New York City. Complete
sets are rare in the United States.

    No attempt is made at the kind of detailed treatment found in the monumental studies
of W. G. Constable, F. J. B. Watson, K. T. Parker, R. Pallucchini and G. F. Guarnati, and
others, although I hope there are some original insights. My purpose has been to sum up
Canaletto's achievements as an etcher, and to include sufficient background on his contri-
butions as a painter to provide a rounded picture of his art. Sizeable and excellent reproductions of all of Canaletto's known etchings are presented for the first time in an American or
English publication.

J.K.

The Etchings of Canaletto

BY JACOB KAINEN

Curator, Division of Graphic Arts

For over two hundred years the glamorous image of 18th-century Venice has been, in large part, the creation of Canaletto. Through his paintings—those remarkable evocations of the tangible physical presence of the city—and through his influence on younger contemporaries such as Bellotto, Marieschi, and Guardi, he has been the main figure in projecting Venice as a subject.

Although Canaletto has been one of the most famous and influential of painters, his reputation as an etcher has not always been high. As late as 1913 Louis R. Metcalfe wrote: "It is not generally known that this prolific painter was also an etcher, and that he produced thirty-two plates which for originality remain unexcelled. That they should have remained so long neglected seems incredible when one realizes their merit . . ."[1]

At first glance the etchings seem quiet and uneventful. They lack the sunny optimism of Canaletto's paintings; they have a different, quite uncharacteristic spirit and a full range of tones that is uncomfortably reminiscent of reproductive etchings after paintings. It is easy to see why they had no strong impact. P. J. Mariette, one of the most knowledgeable connoisseurs of the 18th century, said of the etchings that ". . . la perspective est très bien entendue, mais qui pêchant à mon avis par une touche trop égale et trop peu délicate." (". . . the perspective is well understood but which suffer in my opinion by a monotonous and insensitive handling.")[2] More verve and greater contrasts of light and dark were expected of major etchers both in the 18th and 19th centuries. We can now recognize that Canaletto's prosaic tones were created by unprecedented calligraphic variations, and that the seemingly matter-of-fact vision camouflaged a subtle emotional depth. The tones, in their rhythmic construction, have a transparent, luminous purity. The etchings are now considered among the finest achievements of 18th-century art.

1. "The Etchings of Antonio Canale, called Canaletto (1697–1768)," *The Print Collector's Quarterly*, vol. 3, February 1913, p. 4.

2. *L'Abecedario de P. J. Mariette . . .*, vol. 3, Paris, 1851–1853, p. 298. Mariette died in 1774 and *L'Abecedario* was published much later.

Giovanni Antonio Canal, called Canaletto, was born in Venice on October 18, 1697. He studied with his father Bernardo, a painter of theatrical scenery, from whom he learned the principles of perspective. In 1719 he visited Rome with his father and brother and painted the scenery for Scarlatti's operas *Tito Sempronio Gracco* and *Turno Aricino*. During that period many Flemish and Dutch landscape painters were in Rome, and it seems certain that Canaletto saw their work, particularly that of Gaspar van Wittel, or Vanvitelli as he was known in Italy.[3] Van Wittel had introduced into his scenes of Roman grandeur some of the realism characteristic of town views by Dutch painters, such as Jan van der Heyden and the Berckheyde brothers. Perhaps Canaletto already knew the work of Van Wittel, a former resident of Venice who had produced views of that city in the early 1700s. One thing is certain—the Roman experience marked a turning point for Canaletto. Theatrical design, with its tricks of perspective, no longer satisfied him, and when he returned to Venice in 1720 it was as a landscape painter. Probably he studied briefly with Luca Carlevaris, the first dedicated painter of Venetian views, whose influence at this period was inescapable.[4]

By the 1720s Venice was fully established as the pleasure center of Europe. Lady Mary Wortley Montagu, that extraordinary traveler, noted in 1739 that Venice was the most cosmopolitan of cities, with its high percentage of foreign visitors, and yet it was the least expensive place in Europe. The custom of going about in masks and costumes not only reduced the necessity for wearing expensive gowns but also resulted in "a universal liberty that is certainly one of the greatest *agrémens* [sic] in life . . . it is so much the established fashion for everybody to live their own way . . ."[5]

In this unfettered atmosphere of carnivals, masquerades, and pageantry, it is little wonder that Venice was a city of glamor for cultivated tourists. In its unique charm, its emphasis on

---

3. Op. cit. Mariette, who corresponded with Canaletto, said that he worked "dans la manière de Van Vytel."

4. An article on the etchings of Luca Carlevaris by Campbell Dodgson appeared in *Print Collector's Quarterly*, vol. 17, April, 1930, pp. 155–168.

5. Quoted in Robert Halsband's *The Life of Lady Mary Wortley Montagu*, Oxford, 1956, p. 185.

gaiety, and its water-borne isolation, it was the living embodiment of the 18th-century nostalgia for escape into an irresponsible world of pleasure and dalliance. The world of the *fête galante*, introduced by Antoine Watteau in the early 1700s and epitomized by his island of Cythere, an imaginary pleasureland, was popular throughout the century. But Venice was real, not imaginary; it was a once-powerful city with great traditions in government and the arts. It was, therefore, more than a background for romantic adventure, it was also an educational experience. Not only were there carnivals but magnificent traditional ceremonies as well. Among the most dramatic were those held on the Day of Ascension (May 26) when the Doge was rowed by fifty oarsmen in the Bucintoro (State Barge) to the entrance of the Grand Canal, where he dropped a ring into the water to mark the traditional marriage ceremony between the Republic and the Adriatic.

But the 18th-century Venice was chiefly bent on pleasure. Gambling continued all night on the tables of the Ridotto. Colorful regattas were held along the Grand Canal. Plays by Goldoni and music by Vivaldi—both contemporary Venetians—were included in nightly entertainment. For well-born Englishmen on the Grand Tour, Venice was, in the words of Byron a hundred years later, "a fairy city of the heart." They wanted pictorial mementoes, and no paintings of the city and its pageantry could surpass those of Canaletto. They kept the artist busy with commissions from 1722 until his death in 1768.

Many of the foreign patrons, and chiefly the English, were introduced to the artist by Joseph Smith, a merchant of long standing in Venice who became the British Consul there in 1744.[6] Smith, a collector of books, gems, and works of art, was also an artist's agent and a shrewd businessman. He obtained commissions for Canaletto on behalf of English clients, but apparently the artist did not always welcome the orders. He usually had more work than he

6. Critics have been uncertain of the date on which Smith became the British Consul. Recent writers, following Pallucchini, have accepted the year 1740. But F. J. B. Watson and Ornella Osti have found the exact date, which is June 6, 1744. See W. H. Chaloner, "The Egertons in Italy and the Netherlands," *Bulletin, John Rylands Library*, March, 1950, p. 161.

could handle, and at higher rates.[7] It is easy to understand Horace Walpole's biting reference to Smith as "the Merchant of Venice." But the merchant could be generous as well; he aided the careers of some contemporary artists, sponsored a variety of publications, and collected endlessly. Certainly he was well stocked with Canalettos; in 1763 George III bought from him 54 paintings and 143 drawings by the artist.

In 1746 Canaletto visited England with an introduction from one of his English sponsors, the musical impresario Owen McSwiney. F. J. B. Watson suggests that he was motivated by the desire to keep in contact with his English patrons, who found it almost impossible to travel because of the War of the Austrian Succession.[8] Except for two brief visits to Venice, Canaletto remained in England until 1755 producing, among other subjects, numerous views of London and the country houses of the nobility. His clear, luminous paintings, somewhat colder in tone than his Venetian views, had a strong influence on contemporary English artists and helped to establish the English landscape tradition.

Canaletto's paintings are generally concerned with well-known landmarks, but they also include the teeming life of the city, the markets, workers, and passing crowds. The paintings are remarkable for their illusion of reality. The scenes, drawn in flawless perspective, are flooded with the faintly opalescent sunlight of the city. The colors are rich but finely tempered—a light breeze seems to move through the vistas. The paintings are so convincing in their realism that Canaletto has often been looked on as an unimaginative recorder, or as Cézanne said of Monet, merely an "eye." The fact that he made use of a *camera obscura* or a *camera ottica* has given weight to this charge.[9] The artist made drawings with this mechanical contrivance, which focused an image on paper through a lens and through a series of mirrors, but it is probable that he used this device as a means for gathering material and for noting proportions and perspective lines. This practice was usual for artists from the late 17th century

7. Ibid, pp. 163–164.
8. *Canaletto* (see bibliography), p. 8.
9. Witnessed by A. M. Zanetti (see bibliography), p. 463.

through the 18th. Canaletto's numerous drawings, at Windsor Castle and elsewhere, are generally rough notations made in ink with a broad quill, although, as in the preliminary studies for the etchings, they are sometimes more carefully worked out.[10] But his celebrated realism was not the result of copying what lay before him—it resulted from his ability to organize and project a completely believable image. This required the elimination of distracting elements, the emphasizing of some features and the suppression of others, the invention of necessary forms and accents, and the harmonizing of all into a unified composition.

In giving the impression of an actual view of nature, Canaletto took a long step forward in the art of landscape painting. We must remember that landscapes from the earliest days, through Bellini, Giorgione, and Titian, had been treated as idealized backgrounds for figure subjects. The ideal landscape as a distinct subject was solidly established in the second quarter of the 17th century by Claude Lorrain and Nicolas Poussin, who were intoxicated with antiquity and produced landscapes appropriate to scenes from Homer, Ovid, Vergil, or the Bible. Copying actual trees, hills, and houses was alien to their outlook. Somewhat later in the same period Salvator Rosa treated landscape in a more menacing and picturesque style, often including contemporary figures such as bandits and soldiers, but his treatment of nature was still generalized.

The same principles, now turned into a picture-making formula, were carried over to the 18th century. A new interest in ancient ruins brought subject matter up to date, while suggesting antiquity, and directed some attention to actual forms in nature. The main influence came from Marco Ricci whose heroic landscapes, with their rich color, dramatic chiaroscuro, and contemporary figures and houses, were a distinct modification of earlier ideal views. His example, together with the memory of Claude's luminous skies and Rosa's melodrama were followed by the best of Canaletto's contemporaries, and, in fact, by artists throughout the century.

10. Parker's *The Drawings of Canaletto at Windsor Castle* (see bibliography).

Canaletto's earliest canvases, such as *The Plaza of Saint Mark*, painted before 1723 and now in the Thyssen collection in Lugano, show a tendency to idealization. The background in the Lugano painting is clearly influenced by Luca Carlevaris. But shortly thereafter the younger artist adopted a fresh approach. He abandoned ideal forms and made compositions from observed facts. Probably he felt that Venice did not need idealization. His paintings thereafter seemed to be open windows on nature, even when his subjects were partly invented. The long perspectives, the dramatic contrasts of sunlight and shadow, the play of light on stone and marble, and the clear translucent colors give a trance-like feeling of a moment in time, and we realize that Canaletto is presenting us not with an actual view but with reality as seen in a vivid dream. The living moment is dramatized—the artist has not entirely forgotten his beginnings as a painter of theatrical scenery. But in giving the illusion of an actual place and time, and a feeling of *plein air*, Canaletto gave a new direction to the landscape tradition which foreshadowed 19th century painting from Constable through the impressionists. It was for this reason that he was respected by such later masters as Turner, Constable, and Corot, and revered by Manet and Whistler.

Realistic city views, of course, were painted by the 17th-century Dutch artists, but they lacked Canaletto's vibrant colors, tangible atmosphere, and contrasts of sunlight and shadow, which convey a feeling of immediacy. Except for Vermeer and Saenredam, who painted few city views, they worked with a high finish in a subdued, almost monochrome key. Carlevaris, who founded the tradition of Venetian views, was dry and schematic, although his work has a decorative charm. What Canaletto did was to base himself upon these sources and then trust to his sensations.

About 1740 a change took place in Canaletto's work. Buildings, monuments, bridges, and other details from various sources were arbitrarily combined to create fanciful views, or *vedute ideate*. As his work lost touch with nature his manner became harder, his compositions more contrived. His brushwork, particularly in the figures, became perfunctory—features and garments were suggested with blobs and twists of pigment. But his work of the forties,

although somewhat odd and hybrid in character, still has much to recommend it. His "blob"
technique is certainly original and was carefully noted by other artists, particularly by Guardi.

In the effort to change his outlook after twenty years of Venetian views, Canaletto probably visited Rome in that period. Five paintings of Roman ruins, signed and dated 1742, are in Windsor Castle, together with two dated 1743, and three dated 1744. Another, not at Windsor, is also dated 1744. The Roman views are not always topographically accurate and show some deliberate transpositions of buildings and monuments.

The desire for change, together with a wealth of new architectural forms, may have induced Canaletto to begin etching. The medium was ideally suited for essays in *capricci* and *vedute ideate*, particularly for a superb draftsman with great powers of invention. Black lines on white paper are arbitrary to begin with. The colors of nature are not there to suggest real objects against a real sky, a setting that makes painted *capricci* difficult to believe in. Black and white are a different matter because any objects can be introduced and fitted into a tonal or linear scheme. By dispensing with color, which in invented compositions could be merely decorative and contradictory, the etcher could produce a concentrated and compelling image.

Canaletto might also have been attracted to the new medium by the general revival of interest in etching, and by his continuing association with printmaking workshops in which his paintings and those of other artists were translated into engravings and etchings. Antonio Visentini had completed several engravings after Canaletto's paintings by 1730 which were finally published in a suite of fourteen subjects by Joseph Smith in 1735. By 1742 Smith had added twenty-four plates to round out a publication of thirty-eight views.

The great period of Venetian etching lasted about ten years, from 1740 to 1750, but there were precursors in the century beginning with Luca Carlevaris, who by 1703 had produced 104 views. These etchings were laboriously documentary, in spite of the addition of melodramatic incidents in the foreground. Marco Ricci had etched twenty landscapes, chiefly imaginary, in a spirited style in the 1720s but they were not published until 1730, the year after his death.

The Etchings of Canaletto   In 1741 Michele Marieschi, a painter of views in the Canaletto manner, issued twenty-one highly competent etchings of Venetian landmarks. By 1743 the first great etching suite of the century was published—the ten plates of Giovanni Battista Tiepolo's *Capricci*. These prints, although not views, included landscape details among the brilliant mélange of mysterious elements concerned with death and magic. In the same year the Venetian-bred Giovanni Battista Piranesi published, in Rome, his *Prima Parte di Architettura e Prospettive*; in 1745 his first great set of architectural etchings, the fantastic *Carceri*; and in 1748 his *Antichità romane*. Bernardo Bellotto, Canaletto's nephew and pupil, made his first etchings—eight solidly realized views of Italian cities—by 1747. In the same year Gianfrancesco Costa began work on his charming if somewhat wooden views along the Brenta, following Canaletto's lead, which were published between 1750 and 1756.

On the wave of this general revival of interest in etching, Canaletto began to produce his plates at the age of forty-three or forty-four. Thirty plates were made, some of which were later cut into sections to add up to thirty-four separate prints. Two of these are unique impressions, and one exists in only two impressions. There are four known impressions of the plate for the *Imaginary View of Venice* before it was cut in half (see Checklist), but they are considered a first state, and the separate impressions a second state. In the mid-1740s thirty-one etchings were issued in a bound volume with the following dedication: "Views, some taken from nature, others imaginary, by Antonio Canal, and by him set in perspective, engraved, and dedicated to the most illustrious Joseph Smith, Consul of His Britannic Majesty to the Most Serene Venetian Republic, as a sign of homage and esteem."

It is clear that the dedication plate was made after June 6, 1744, the date on which Smith became Consul. No doubt it was the final plate since it refers to a series of prints already created. It is likely, therefore, that the bound volume of thirty-one etchings was published between the dates of Smith's appointment as Consul and 1746, when the artist made his first visit to England.

CANALETTO Preparatory drawing for *Imaginary View of Venice* (P & G 12). British Museum, London.

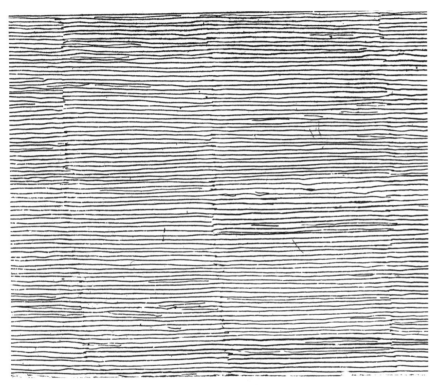

Detail of sky, enlarged. Canaletto, *Village on the Banks of a River*.

Detail of sky, enlarged. Marco Ricci, *A Village*.

CANALETTO Preparatory drawing for *Imaginary View of Venice* (P & G 12). British Museum, London.

Detail of sky, enlarged. Canaletto, *Village on the Banks of a River*.

Detail of sky, enlarged. Marco Ricci, *A Village*.

Canaletto's etchings, with few exceptions, are not concerned with the famous landmarks of Venice. Some show the more humble, everyday aspects of the city, the little byways, and the banks of the Brenta River as far as Padua; others are *capricci*, or fantasies, composed of humble dwellings, wild landscapes, and desolate palaces, statues, and bridges. A sober, elegiac mood prevails.

From his first plate it was evident that Canaletto was a supreme master of the medium. Certain influences are present, but they are absorbed in the larger unity of the artist's highly personal vision. There is no doubt that he was aware of Marco Ricci's treatment of skies, which were rendered in tiers of short, light, horizontal lines which produced a flicker at their joinings. Canaletto's trees, also, have a certain Riccian twist. The figures, in their strong linear treatment, suggest that the etcher had looked at Jacques Callot. But the influences are hardly significant. The dominant characteristic of the etchings, as of the paintings, is the play of light on the various surfaces of buildings, trees, and terrain. To achieve this result Canaletto conceived his compositions in terms of tonal values with the main forms, usually the buildings, standing out in luminous and modulated white, with dark areas in the foreground and middle distance to bring the lights out still further. The tones were created by a simple system of shading in parallel lines which were often applied in a sort of controlled tremor to create a vibrant, atmospheric feeling of light and misty heat. The dark masses were composed of thick, sinuous lines with enough white showing between the lines to reveal the forms and to give them a feeling of reflected light. Foliage was treated in little, decisively hooked strokes, strongly etched, which emphasized the artist's essentially calligraphic draftsmanship.

The variety in Canaletto's groups of parallel lines is astonishing. They move lightly and serenely, they twist in violent short arcs, they join at intervals to enclose little pools of light, and they make patches of tone by being set at right angles to each other. The directness and freshness of his style indicate that he did not worry his plates with extensive stoppings out and rebitings. Maria Pittaluga[11] has suggested that Canaletto used no more than one or two

11. "Le acqueforti del Canaletto," L'Arte, July, 1934.

immersions in the acid, a procedure that would be possible if he employed several needles varying in thickness to draw through the etching ground. The tones could then be systematically determined by the thickness of the needles and the spaces between the lines. Clearly he used a separate wide needle with a flat point for accents and for the darkest areas, and we can reasonably suppose that he used other points.

It is unusual for an artist to show such complete technical mastery in his first etchings, particularly when dealing with complex problems of modulated light. His achievement is remarkable if, in addition, he invents a personal method. But we know that Canaletto, in his vast output of drawings, was accustomed to suggesting tones through the use of lines. Working through the dark etching ground with a blunt needle which slid over the polished copper in response to his most wayward impulse, his draftsman's instinct was heightened. When he created tones he did not render them mechanically; he drew them with a vivid sense of form and rhythm. When he failed, as he did occasionally, as in the two *Prà della Valle* etchings, it was because his subjects were barren and gave him little scope for invention.

About eleven prints describe actual localities—the others are inventions, although at times it is difficult to distinguish the real from the imaginary, and a strange mood is created in which reality and unreality are combined. The views from nature are marked off from the rest by being titled, and with some exceptions they are the least inspired. Famous landmarks are included, but, generally speaking, the less famous the subject the better the print.

The earliest six views, from *Ale Porte del Dolo* to *Prà della Valle* (P & G 2 through 7),[12] are more or less direct transcriptions from nature, suffused, to be sure, with Canaletto's poetry and with his invented happenings. Probably the finest of this group are the first two, *Ale Porte del Dolo*, which shows a covered pleasure boat in the shadowed foreground and sunlit buildings across the river, and *le Porte del Dolo*, with its diagonal shadow across the canal lock, its contrast of patricians and workers, and its marvelous control of tones. With the seventh landscape, *la Torre di Malghera* (P & G 8) (torn down in the mid-1830s), a new quality comes

---

12. The initials P & G refer to Pallucchini and Guarnati's catalog. See Checklist.

CANALETTO Preparatory drawing for *Village on the Banks of a River* (P & G 9). Windsor Castle, Royal Library. By gracious permission of Her Majesty Queen Elizabeth II.

CANALETTO Preparatory drawing for *Al Dolo* (P & G 4). Victoria and Albert Museum, London.

into the etchings. The compositions become less crowded, the emotional tone intensifies, and the technical handling becomes looser and more rhythmical. The subjects are either partially or completely inventions with the exception of two market views (P & G 19 and 21) and four small, comparatively prosaic scenes in St. Mark's Square (P & G 14 through 17). *Le Preson V* and *le Procuratie nioue e S. Ziminian V* are probably the most effective of the four, but *la Piera del Bando V* is of particular interest because it shows an old custom—the Comandador announcing government decrees from the traditional stone pedestal. The series from P & G 9 through 21 includes Canaletto's finest etchings, beginning with *Village on the Banks of a River*, with its expressive tree in the foreground, its transparent atmosphere, and its mood of strange quiet. Probably the most dramatic of the inventions is *Portico with a Lantern* (P & G 11), in which a portion of the sky is kept white to dramatize the dark, neglected lantern, which hangs like a threatening weight. The magnificent *Imaginary View of Venice: House with the Inscription* (P & G 12a) bears in a conspicuous area the notation "MDCCXLI. A.C." This is the only dated print.

With *Landscape with a Pilgrim Praying* (P & G 22) another change takes place. Canaletto's execution becomes more direct and forceful and his subjects less topographical. He seems no longer interested in rendering nature—he merely suggests it with swift, live strokes. As his style broadens, the humanism implicit in the previous etchings becomes more specific. *Landscape with a Pilgrim Praying*, for example, shows a pilgrim at a wayside shrine, a precarious bridge, a rugged uphill path, and a building in ruins. *Alpine Landscape with Three Bridges* (P & G 25) shows travelers in wagons and on foot crossing flimsy bridges over gorges in a swaying landscape, while a wanderer rests in the foreground. A man hanging from a gibbet is barely discernible against a background of foliage.

After his brief but concentrated excursion into etching, Canaletto never returned to the medium. Perhaps it is more than a coincidence that few, if any, of the first-rate Venetian painters of his time produced more than a small body of prints. Working in a new medium the artists had little interest in repeating their paintings; they created fresh ideas in terms of

The Etchings of Canaletto

printmaking. Obviously these uncharacteristic prints did not appeal to a largely transient audience interested in the color, glamor, and gaiety of Venice. For such artists as Ricci, Canaletto, Marieschi, the Tiepolos, and Bellotto, the long hours of work on copper plates, involving innumerable proofings and re-etchings, brought incommensurate financial returns. The public was more interested in reproductions of their paintings, which could be made by professional engravers. It was probably with this realization that Canaletto, when he returned from England, was content to supply paintings and drawings to be reproduced by the engraver and publisher Giuseppe Wagner, and by the engraver Giambattista Brustolon for the publisher Furlanetto.

Although Canaletto's career as an etcher was short, it was on the highest level. His prints remain a remarkable achievement, not only because they are technically unsurpassed, but also because they show the grace and clarity of the rational mind overlaid with the irrational fancies that come only in dreams and visions. The commonplace is invested with a lonely grandeur through which we glimpse a deep concern for the meaning of physical decay and spiritual isolation. The fact that this concern is not immediately evident, that it is incorporated in a natural drama of sunlight and shadow, gives these prints several levels of meaning and places them among the masterpieces of etching.

Selected Bibliography

De Vesme, Alexandre, *Le Peintre Graveur Italien*, Milan, 1906.

Constable, W. G., *Canaletto: Giovanni Antonio Canal*, Oxford, 1962. 2 vols.

Garson, Inez, *Canaletto: The Etchings*, introduction to catalog of exhibition at the Andrew Dickson White Art Gallery, Cornell University, Ithaca, New York, 1963.

Pallucchini, Rodolfo, and Guarnati, G. F., *Le acqueforti del Canaletto*, Venice, 1945.

Parker, K. T., *The Drawings of Canaletto at Windsor Castle*, Oxford and London, 1948.

Watson, F. J. B., *Canaletto*, London, 1949.

Weinhardt, Carl J., Jr., "Canaletto: Master Etcher," *The Metropolitan Museum of Art Bulletin*, November 1958.

Zanetti, A. M., *Della pittura veneziana*, Venice, 1771.

Checklist

The first reliable catalog of Canaletto's etchings was published by De Vesme in 1906, but it was superseded in 1945 by the exhaustive and definitive work of Pallucchini and Guarnati, to which grateful acknowledgement is made. To attempt another full catalog, as W. G. Constable said in a similar situation, ". . . would be superfluous and almost an impertinence." Nevertheless Constable has provided valuable descriptions of the etchings (see bibliography, v. 2) and a full list of engravers and engravings after Canaletto. I gratefully acknowledge a debt to him also.

The numbers before the titles refer to Pallucchini and Guarnati's catalog. The titles in quotation marks are those lettered on the plates by Canaletto. The measurements, which include full traces of the platemarks, are in inches and sixteenths, with the vertical dimensions given first. The prints marked with an asterisk (*) were not included in the published volume of the etchings and represent unique or scarce impressions.

Later editions, which usually include twenty-five etchings when in bound volumes, have ten prints with added letters and numbers such as "F F 1," "E 1," etc. They are noted in the following checklist.

In preparing his plates Canaletto followed a definite format. The first eleven prints are about 12 x 17 inches, with allowances made for slight variations because of paper shrinkage. The next two prints are halves of the preceding size, and the remainder are quarters. Exceptions are the three sections of *View of a Town with the Tomb of a Bishop* (P & G 13a, b, c) and the two parts of *Landscape with a Bridge and a Little Monument* (P & G 29a, b), which Canaletto apparently cut up for reasons of design. The plates cannot be examined because they disappeared shortly after his death. Cicogna,[13] relying upon a distant memory, said he was told that they were sold to a London merchant.

Many prints from old collections still bear De Vesme catalog numbers, and I have therefore included them in the checklist.

13. *Della Iscrizione Veneziane*, vol. v, Venice, 1842.

P & G No.

1. Frontispiece: "VEDUTE / Altre prese da i Luoghi altre ideate / DA / ANTONIO CANAL / e da esso intagliate poste in prospetiva / umiliate / All' Illmo Signor / GIUSEPPE SMITH / Console di S. M. Britanica appresso la Ser.^{mo} Repubblica di Venezia. / In segno di stima ed ossequio"

The figures to the right suggest Piranesi, and, surprisingly, Salvator Rosa.
11.13 × 16.13
De V. 1

2. "Ale Porte del Dolo"

The pleasure boat is leaving the main canal of Dolo and entering the Brenta River, which connects Venice and Padua.

11.15 × 17.1
Later impressions have "F F 1" in the lower margin.
De V. 5

3. "le Porte del Dolo"

The canal lock at Dolo, with closed gates, and a view of the Brenta.
11.14 × 17.1
Later impressions have "F F 2" in the lower margin.
De V. 6

4. "Al Dolo"

The town of Dolo looking west from the right bank of the Brenta. The Church of S. Rocco is to the right.

11.14×17
Later impressions have "F F 3" in the lower margin.
De V. 4

5. "Mestre"

A panoramic view of Mestre with the Canale delle Barche in the center.
11.14×17.1
Later impressions have "E 1" in the lower margin.
De V. 3

6. "S.a Giustina in prà della Vale"

The Prato della Valle in Padua, with the Church of S. Giustina. This print forms a continuous view with "Prà della Valle" (P & G 7), which follows.
11.14×17
Later impressions have "E 2" in the lower margin.
De V. 8

7. "Prà della Valle"

A continuation of the preceding view (P & G 6).
11.14×17
Later impressions have "E 3" in the lower margin.
De V. 7

8. "la Torre di Malghera"

The Tower of Marghera, built in a lagoon near Mestre, guarded the northern approaches to Venice. It was torn down in the mid-1830s.

11.14×17.1
Later impressions have "E 4" in the lower margin.
De V. 2

9. Village on the Banks of a River

The exact location is not certain. Pallucchini believes the place to be Padua along the Brenta. The center tree shows some influence of Marco Ricci and Salvator Rosa.
11.13×17
Later impressions have "E 5" in the lower margin.
De V. 9

10. Imaginary View of Padua

Meyer considers this a view of Murano, but P & G believe it resembles Padua altered to create a *veduta ideata*.
11.14×17.1
Later impressions have "E 6" in the lower margin.
De V. 11

11. Portico with a Lantern

This imaginary composition combines invented architectural forms, vaguely Roman, with a distant view of a lagoon.
11.15×17.1
Later impressions have "F F 4" on the terrain to the lower left. In still later impressions "F F 4" is removed and is replaced by "E."
De V. 10

*12. Imaginary View of Venice

This *veduta ideate*, which has a dreamlike irrationality, combines echoes of Venice and Rome.
11.15 × 17.3
Impression from the complete plate before it was cut in half to form 12a and 12b. P & G knew only three examples of this first state, one of which is in this country at the Fogg Museum, Cambridge. Constable has discovered a fourth impression at the Courtauld Institute, London.
De V. 12–13

12a. Imaginary View of Venice: The House with the Inscription

11.15 × 8.11
The left half of the divided plate. The house to the left bears the inscription "MDCCXLI. A. C."
2nd state, together with 12b.
De V. 12

12b. Imaginary View of Venice: The House with the Colonnade

11.13 × 8.7
The right half of the divided plate.
2nd state, together with 12a. In the lower margin, right: "A.C."
De V. 13

13a. View of a Town with the Tomb of a Bishop: Fragments of Sculpture

8.11 × 5.2
This imaginary composition is the upper left section of a plate that was cut into three parts. P & G say that in the first printing 13a appears on a single sheet between 29a and 29b; in the second it appears to the left followed by 29a and 29b.
De V. 29

13b. View of a Town with the Tomb of a Bishop: The Tomb of a Bishop

11.13 × 11.15
This is the right-hand section of the three-part plate.
De V. 14

*13c. View of a Town with the Tomb of a Bishop: Fragment

3.2 × 5.2
The only known impression is in an album at Windsor Castle.
Not in De V.

14. "le Preson. V."

The old prison is connected to the Ducal Palace by the Bridge of Sighs.
5.12 × 8.6
De V. 18

15. "la Libreria. V."

The Library of St. Mark, designed by Sansovino, and a view of the Piazzetta.
5.12 × 8.5
De V. 15

16. "le Procuratie nioue e S. Ziminian V."

A view in the Piazza S. Marco with the Procu-

ratie Nuove to the left and the Church of San Geminiano in the background.
5.9×8.7
De V. 22

17. "la Piera del Bando. V."

The stone pedestal in the Piazza S. Marco from which government laws were proclaimed. A closer view of the stone appears to the left in P & G 15.
5.12×8.5
De V. 16

18. The Terrace

A terrace facing a courtyard. The subject seems based on nature, with Canaletto's usual modifications.
5.12×8.9
De V. 21

19. The Market at Dolo

The market is in front of the portico of the Church of S. Rocco. The distant hill is invented.
5.12×8.9
De V. 23

20. Imaginary View of S. Giacomo di Rialto

A *capriccio* based upon the Church of S. Giacomo di Rialto. The statue and columns are imaginary.
5.12×8.7
De V. 27

21. Market on the Molo

The Molo is the docking area of the island of S. Giorgio Maggiore. The dome and roof of S. Giorgio appear in the background. The entire view is reversed.
5.12×8.6
De V. 17

22. Landscape with a Pilgrim Praying

An imaginary composition with humanistic overtones. This print marks a change in Canaletto to a generally sketchier treatment.
5.9×8.5
De V. 24

23. Landscape with Equestrian Monument

A *capriccio* dominated by an equestrian statue. A catafalque is in the center.
5.12×8.5
De V. 20

24. Landscape with Woman Pumping Water

An imaginary composition, probably the most freely treated of all the etchings. The initials "A. C." are etched so faintly in the terrain at the lower left that they rarely appear in reproductions.
5.9×8.5
De V. 26

25. Alpine Landscape with Three Bridges

An imaginary subject with humanistic overtones. A hanged man is barely visible at the right edge, center.
5.12×8.6
De V. 19

26. Landscape with Monuments in Ruins

A *capriccio* based on Roman themes.
5.12×8.9
De V. 28

27. Landscape with Dungeon and Two Columns in Ruins

An imaginary composition with echoes of Padua.
5.9×8.5
De V. 25

*28. Landscape with a Church, Houses, and a Mill

An imaginary composition dominated by a church in the background.
5.12×8.4
Only two impressions are known, one at the Berlin Kupferstichkabinett and the other at Windsor Castle.
De V. 32

29a. Landscape with a Bridge and a Little Monument: Cart Crossing a Bridge

An imaginary subject.
5.11×5

This is the left section of a plate which was cut to form two subjects. The other section is 29b. (For additional data see 13a).
De V. 31

29b. Landscape with a Bridge and a Little Monument: The Little Monument under a Tree

The right section of the plate, continuing the subject in 29a but with the upper part cut off.
4.11×3.5
De V. 30

*30. Alpine Landscape with a Church, Houses, and Two Columns

An imaginary composition, classically composed. A strong diagonal movement from upper left to lower right is counterbalanced by two short opposing diagonals. A circular movement connecting sky with terrain is in the center. Two strong verticals on the right give stability to the composition.
5.12×8.3
Unique impression at Windsor Castle.

VEDUTE
Altre prese da i Luoghi altre ideate
DA
ANTONIO CANAL
e da esso intagliate poste in prospetiva
umiliate
All' Ill.mo Signor

GIUSEPPE SMITH
Console di S. M. Britanica appresso la Ser.
Repubblica di Venezia.
In segno di stima ed ossequio

1. Frontispiece

A. Canal F.   Ale Porte del Dolo.

2. "Ale Porte del Dolo"

A. Canal F.   le Porte Del Dolo

3. "le Porte del Dolo"

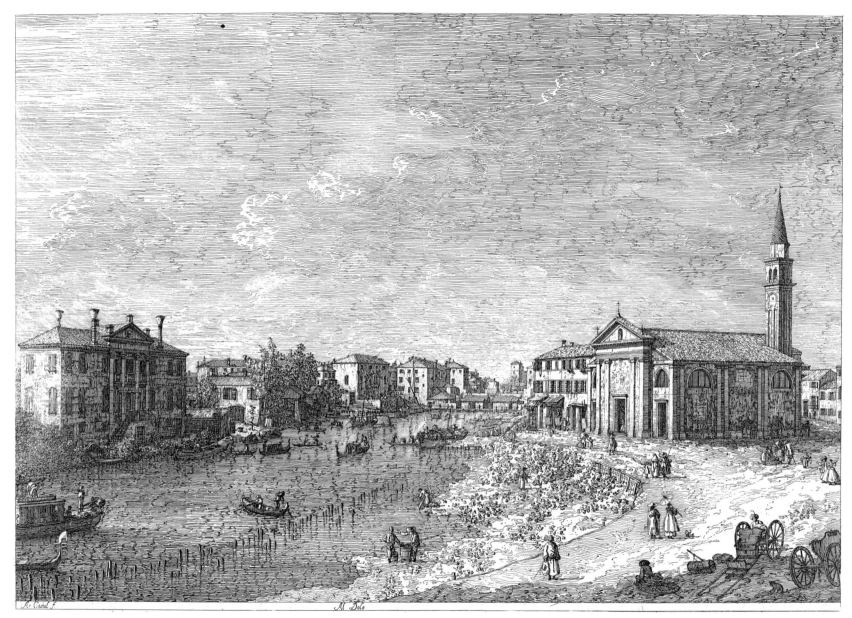

4. "Al Dolo"

A. Canal f.   Mestre

5. "Mestre"

A. Canal f.   S.a Giustina in prà della Vale

6. "S.a Giustina in prà della Vale"

A. Canal f.   Prà della Valle

7. "Prà della Valle"

A. Canal f.   la Torre di Malghera

8. "la Torre di Malghera"

8. Detail.

A. Canal f.

9. Village on the Banks of a River

A. Canal f.

10. Imaginary View of Padua

11. Portico with a Lantern

*12. Imaginary View of Venice

MDCCXLIAC

12a. Imaginary View of Venice: The House with the Inscription

12b. Imaginary View of Venice: The House with the Colonnade

Left 13a. View of a Town with the Tomb of a Bishop: Fragments of Sculpture

Right 13b. View of a Town with the Tomb of a Bishop: The Tomb of a Bishop

*13c. View of a Town with the Tomb of a Bishop: Fragment

A. Canal f.   le Preson. V.

14. "le Preson. V."

A. Canal. f.   la Libreria. V.

15. "la Libreria. V".

A. Canal. F.   le Procuratie nioue e S. Ziminian V.

16. "le Procuratie nioue e S. Ziminian V."

A. Canal. f.   la Piera del Bando. V.

17. "la Piera del Bando. V."

18. The Terrace

A. Canal. f.

19. The Market at Dolo

A. Canal f.

20. Imaginary View of S. Giacomo di Rialto

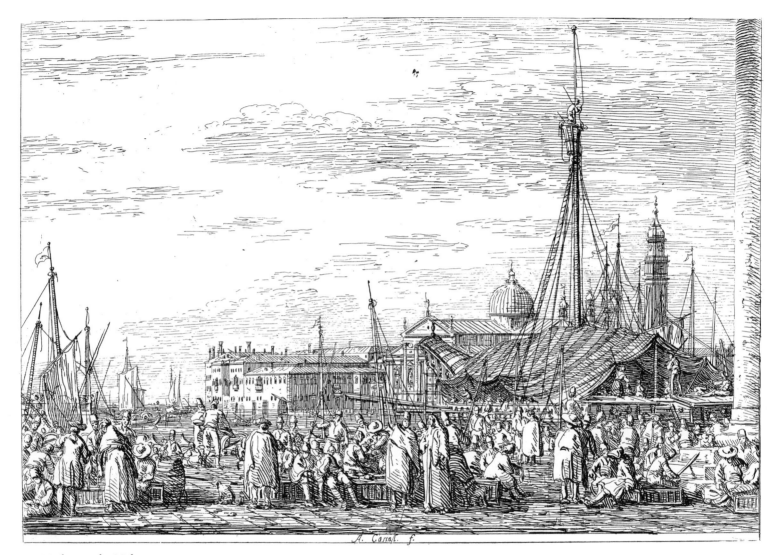

21. Market on the Molo

A. Canal. F.

22. Landscape with a Pilgrim Praying

23. Landscape with Equestrian Monument

24. Landscape with Woman Pumping Water

A. Canal f.

25. Alpine Landscape with Three Bridges

A. Canal f.

26. Landscape with Monuments in Ruins

27. Landscape with Dungeon and Two Columns in Ruins

A. Canal f.

*28. Landscape with a Church, Houses, and a Mill

29a. Landscape with a Bridge and a Little Monument:
Cart Crossing a Bridge

29b. Landscape with a Bridge and a Little Monument:
The Little Monument under a Tree

A. Canal. f.

*30. Alpine Landscape with a Church, Houses, and Two Columns